TikTok Triumph: The Ultimate Guide to Monetizing Your Creativity in 2024

Welcome to the TikTok Revolution

Welcome to the TikTok Revolution! In the fast-paced world of social media, TikTok has emerged as a powerhouse, capturing the attention of millions worldwide. What sets TikTok apart is its emphasis on short-form, engaging content that allows creators to showcase their talents, creativity, and unique perspectives. This guide is your key to unlocking the potential of TikTok and turning your passion into profit. Whether you're a seasoned TikTok user or just starting, the possibilities for monetizing your creativity are endless.

1: Understanding the TikTok Landscape

- Unveiling the TikTok Algorithm: Learn how TikTok's algorithm works and how to leverage it to increase visibility and engagement for your content.

- Navigating Trends: Explore the latest trends and challenges on TikTok, understanding how to incorporate them into your content strategy to stay relevant and attract a wider audience.

2: Building Your Personal Brand

- Crafting a Unique Identity: Define your niche and establish a distinctive personal brand that resonates with your target audience.

- Optimizing Your Profile: Learn the art of creating an eye-catching TikTok profile, complete with a compelling bio, profile picture, and links to your other social media platforms.

3: Content Creation Mastery

- Video Production Tips: Dive into the techniques that make TikTok videos stand out, from effective editing to using popular effects and filters.

- Storytelling on TikTok: Master the art of storytelling in short-form videos, capturing your audience's attention and keeping them engaged from start to finish.

4: Monetization Strategies

- TikTok Creator Fund: Explore the TikTok Creator Fund and discover how you can earn money directly from TikTok based on your content's performance.

- Brand Partnerships: Learn how to collaborate with brands and secure sponsored deals, turning your TikTok presence into a lucrative source of income.
- Selling Merchandise: Explore the world of e-commerce by designing and selling your merchandise directly through TikTok.

5: Legal and Safety Considerations
- Copyright and Fair Use: Understand the legal aspects of content creation, ensuring that your videos comply with copyright laws and fair use policies.
- Online Safety: Protect yourself and your audience by implementing best practices for online safety and maintaining a positive and secure TikTok environment.

The Power of Short-form Content

Short-form content has proven to be a powerful and influential force in the digital landscape, with platforms like TikTok leading the way in revolutionizing how we consume and create content. The power of short-form content lies in its ability to capture attention quickly, deliver a message concisely, and engage audiences in a way that fits seamlessly into today's fast-paced, on-the-go lifestyle.

Here are some key aspects highlighting the power of short-form content:

1. Attention Span Economy: In an era where attention spans are increasingly shorter, short-form content excels at grabbing and maintaining viewers' attention. Users can quickly scroll through a feed and consume multiple short videos in a short amount of time, making it more likely for creators to reach a wider audience.

2. Accessibility and Inclusivity: Short-form content is accessible to a wide range of people, regardless of their internet speed or device capabilities. This inclusivity contributes to the democratization of content creation, allowing creators from diverse backgrounds to share their perspectives and creativity.

3. Viral Potential: The bite-sized nature of short-form content makes it highly shareable. A captivating video can quickly go viral, reaching a massive audience in a short period. This virality contributes to the rapid growth of creators' profiles and the potential for increased visibility and opportunities.

4. Creative Expression in a Snap: Short-form content platforms often provide a plethora of creative tools, filters, and effects that allow creators to express themselves in unique and visually appealing ways. The low barrier to entry encourages experimentation, fostering a creative environment where innovation thrives.

5. Trend Participation: Short-form content platforms are known for their trend-centric culture. Creators can leverage existing trends or create their own, capitalizing on the platform's algorithm that often promotes content related to popular trends. This dynamic environment keeps content fresh and engaging.

6. Monetization Opportunities: As these platforms mature, they introduce various monetization features for content creators. From brand partnerships and sponsored content to direct creator funds and ad revenue sharing, short-form content creators can now turn their passion into a sustainable income stream.

7. Global Reach: Short-form content has the potential to transcend language and cultural barriers, allowing creators to reach a global audience. This broad reach opens up new opportunities for collaboration, cultural exchange, and the creation of content with universal appeal.

Why TikTok in 2024?

1. User Base and Engagement: TikTok has consistently attracted a massive and diverse user base, including people of various age groups, interests, and backgrounds. The platform's algorithm, which delivers personalized content to users based on their preferences, contributes to high engagement levels.

2. Short-Form Content Dominance: TikTok's success is closely tied to its emphasis on short-form video content. In a world where attention spans are diminishing, the platform's 15 to 60-second video format provides a quick and entertaining way for users to consume content.

3. Creative Expression and Trends: TikTok has become a hub for creative expression, enabling users to showcase their talents, creativity, and humor. The platform's trend-centric nature keeps content fresh and encourages users to participate in viral challenges, dances, and other trends.

4. Algorithmic Advantage: TikTok's recommendation algorithm is known for its effectiveness in surfacing content tailored to users' preferences. This personalized content discovery mechanism has contributed significantly to the platform's rapid growth and user retention.

5. Innovative Features: TikTok continually introduces new features and tools to keep its user experience exciting. From interactive elements like duets and stitching to creative filters and effects, these features enhance user engagement and contribute to the platform's popularity.

6. Global Cultural Impact: TikTok has become a global cultural phenomenon, influencing trends, music, and internet culture on a massive scale. The platform's ability to facilitate the rapid spread of content and trends across borders has contributed to its cultural significance.

7. Monetization Opportunities: TikTok has been actively working on providing monetization opportunities for its creators. This includes the TikTok Creator Fund, live gifts, brand partnerships, and more. In 2024, these monetization channels may have evolved, offering creators additional ways to earn income from their content.

8. Adoption by Brands and Celebrities: Many brands and celebrities have recognized the reach and impact of TikTok, leading to increased collaboration and marketing efforts on the platform. TikTok's ability to turn regular users into influencers and trendsetters has made it an attractive space for brands to connect with their target audience.

It's essential to check the latest information to understand the specific developments and trends on TikTok in 2024. The platform's continued success will likely hinge on its ability to adapt to changing user behaviors, introduce innovative features, and maintain a vibrant and engaging community.

Understanding TikTok

Key Features:

1. Short-Form Videos: TikTok is primarily known for short-form videos, ranging from 15 to 60 seconds. This format encourages concise, engaging, and easily consumable content.

2. For You Page (FYP): The FYP is the main feed on TikTok, where the algorithm showcases content based on user preferences, interactions, and trends. It's designed to introduce users to a diverse range of content.

3. Trends and Challenges: TikTok thrives on trends and challenges. Users often participate in popular challenges, dances, and memes, contributing to a dynamic and ever-evolving content landscape.

4. Duets and Stitching: Users can create collaborative content through duets, where they react to or perform alongside another user's video. Stitching allows users to integrate a segment of someone else's video into their own.

5. Creative Tools: TikTok provides an array of creative tools such as filters, effects, text overlays, and a diverse music library. These tools empower users to enhance and personalize their content.

6. Live Streaming: Users with a certain number of followers can go live on TikTok, engaging with their audience in real-time. Viewers can send virtual gifts to support their favorite creators during live sessions.

7. Engagement Metrics: TikTok allows users to see the number of views, likes, comments, and shares on their videos. The engagement metrics play a crucial role in determining the popularity of content.

8. Privacy Settings: Users can customize their privacy settings, controlling who can comment on their videos, duet with them, or view their content. This flexibility enhances user control over their TikTok experience.

TikTok Culture:

1. Diversity and Inclusivity: TikTok's user base is diverse, welcoming creators from various backgrounds and talents. This inclusivity has contributed to the platform's global appeal.

2. Authenticity: TikTok values authenticity, with users often showcasing genuine moments, talents, and relatable content. This contrasts with the polished and curated content found on some other platforms.

3. Community Engagement: TikTok fosters a sense of community where users engage through comments, duets, and collaborations. The interactive nature of the platform strengthens connections among creators and their audience.

4. Rapid Virality: TikTok's algorithm can rapidly propel content to viral status, allowing users to gain widespread recognition quickly. This has led to the rise of "TikTok celebrities" who gain fame through the platform.

5. Cultural Impact: TikTok has had a profound impact on music, fashion, and internet culture. Trends originating on TikTok often influence broader pop culture.

TikTok in Business:

1. Brand Partnerships: Many brands collaborate with TikTok creators for marketing campaigns, leveraging the influencers' reach and creativity.

2. Advertising: TikTok offers advertising options for businesses, allowing them to reach a vast and engaged user base through sponsored content and in-feed ads.

3. E-commerce Integration: TikTok has explored e-commerce features, allowing users to shop directly through the platform. Understanding TikTok involves recognizing its unique blend of creativity, community, and trends. As the platform continues to evolve, staying informed about new features and cultural shifts will be essential for anyone looking to engage with TikTok effectively.

The Algorithm Unveiled

While the exact details of TikTok's algorithm are proprietary and not fully disclosed by the company, some aspects of how it works have been revealed based on observations and statements from TikTok itself. Here's a simplified understanding of TikTok's algorithm:

1. For You Page (FYP): The centerpiece of TikTok's algorithm is the For You Page (FYP). When users open the app, they are taken directly to the FYP, a personalized feed curated by the algorithm. The content on the FYP is not determined by who the user follows but rather by the algorithm's assessment of the user's preferences.

2. Machine Learning and User Interaction: TikTok employs machine learning to analyze user behavior and interactions within the app. The algorithm considers a variety of factors, such as the types of content users engage with (like, share, comment), the accounts they follow, and the time spent watching each video.

3. Video Information: The algorithm takes into account details about each video, including captions, hashtags, sounds, and effects used. It looks for patterns and similarities between videos that users engage with to refine content recommendations.

4. Device and Account Settings: TikTok's algorithm also considers device and account settings, including language preference, country location, and device type. This helps tailor content to users based on their regional and language preferences.

5. Engagement Patterns: The algorithm looks at how users engage with different types of content. If a user consistently engages with videos of a certain style or theme, the algorithm is more likely to recommend similar content.

6. Freshness of Content: TikTok values fresh and recently uploaded content. The algorithm aims to keep the content on users' FYPs current and relevant, promoting videos that are trending or have gained sudden popularity.

7. Diversity of Content: TikTok's algorithm strives to provide users with a diverse range of content. Even if a user has specific interests, the algorithm introduces variety to keep the browsing experience interesting and prevent users from getting stuck in a content bubble.

8. Duets and Stitching: The ability to create duets and stitches (split-screen collaborations with other videos) contributes to the virality of content. These features allow users to interact with and build upon existing content, creating a network effect.

Remember that TikTok's algorithm is dynamic and continually evolves based on user behavior and platform developments. As a result, users may find their content preferences changing over time as the algorithm refines its understanding of their interests. TikTok's commitment to user personalization and discovery is a key factor in its widespread popularity.

Building Your TikTok Brand

Crafting a Captivating Profile

Crafting a captivating profile on TikTok is essential for making a strong first impression and attracting and retaining followers. Here are some tips to help you create an engaging and memorable TikTok profile:

1. Profile Picture:
   - Choose a clear and high-quality profile picture.
   - Use an image that represents your brand or personality.
   - Ensure your face or brand logo is easily recognizable, even in a small thumbnail.

2. Username:
   - Keep your username short, memorable, and reflective of your brand or content niche.
   - Avoid using special characters or numbers that may be hard to remember.
   - Ensure it's unique and not easily confused with other accounts.

3. Bio:
   - Craft a concise and attention-grabbing bio.

- Clearly state your interests, niche, or the type of content you create.
- Use emojis to add personality and break up text.
- Include relevant keywords to help users find your profile through searches.

4. Link:
- If you have a website, YouTube channel, or other social media accounts, add a link to your bio.
- Consider using a link shortener to keep the bio tidy and visually appealing.
- Use the link to direct users to additional content or platforms related to your brand.

5. Featured TikToks:
- Take advantage of the "Featured" section to showcase your best and most representative TikToks.
- Choose videos that highlight your creativity, personality, or popular content.
- Regularly update the featured videos to keep the content fresh.

6. Consistent Aesthetic:
- Maintain a consistent aesthetic in your profile pictures, cover photos, and featured videos.
- Choose a color scheme or theme that aligns with your brand or content style.

7. Engagement Metrics:
- Display your follower count, following count, and likes if you're comfortable.
- High engagement metrics can create social proof and attract more followers.
- Alternatively, you can keep these private if you prefer a cleaner look.

8. Connect with Trends:
- Participate in current trends and challenges to show that your content is current and relevant.
- Use trending hashtags in your bio to increase discoverability.

9. Duets and Stitches:
- Enable duets and stitches to encourage collaboration with other creators.
- This can enhance engagement and showcase your willingness to interact with your audience.

10. Live Streaming:
   - If you frequently go live, mention your live schedule in the bio to notify followers when they can catch you in real-time.
   - Highlight any special events or topics you cover during live streams.

11. Personality and Tone:
   - Infuse your personality into your bio and profile elements.
   - Use a conversational tone that resonates with your target audience.

Remember, your TikTok profile is a snapshot of who you are and what you create. Make it visually appealing, informative, and aligned with your brand to capture the attention of potential followers and keep them engaged with your content.

Finding Your Niche

Finding your niche on TikTok is a crucial step in building a focused and engaged audience. Here are some steps to help you discover and define your niche on the platform:

1. Identify Your Interests:
   - List out your hobbies, passions, and interests.
   - Consider what topics genuinely excite and inspire you.

2. Evaluate Your Skills:
   - Assess your skills and expertise in various areas.
   - Identify what you're knowledgeable about or eager to learn.

3. Explore TikTok Trends:
   - Spend time on TikTok exploring different content categories.
   - Take note of trending hashtags, challenges, and popular niches.

4. Analyze Your Audience:
   - Consider who you want to target with your content.
   - Think about the demographics, interests, and preferences of your ideal audience.

5. Research Competitors:
   - Look at what other creators in your potential niches are doing.
   - Identify gaps or areas where you can offer a unique perspective or content style.

6. Define Your Unique Angle:
   - Think about what makes you unique and how you can stand out.
   - Consider your personality, background, or a specific approach that sets you apart.

7. Test Different Content:

- Experiment with creating content in various niches.
- Pay attention to which types of content resonate most with your audience.

8. Gather Feedback:
- Encourage feedback from your audience through comments and messages.
- Use feedback to understand what your audience appreciates and what they want to see more of.

9. Narrow Down Your Focus:
- Based on your exploration and feedback, narrow down your focus to a specific niche.
- Aim for a niche that aligns with your interests, skills, and audience preferences.

10. Consistency is Key:
- Be consistent in the type of content you produce within your chosen niche.
- Establish a recognizable style that viewers can associate with your brand.

11. Adapt and Evolve:
- Stay open to adapting your content based on trends and audience feedback.
- Be willing to evolve within your niche to keep your content fresh and engaging.

12. Authenticity Matters:
- Ensure that your chosen niche aligns with your authentic self.
- Authenticity resonates with viewers and contributes to building a genuine connection with your audience.

Remember that finding your niche is an ongoing process, and it's okay to evolve as you learn more about what works best for you and your audience. By combining your interests, skills, and a unique perspective, you can create a niche that not only resonates with you but also attracts a dedicated and engaged TikTok audience.

Content Strategies for Success

To achieve success on TikTok, it's essential to employ effective content strategies that capture audience attention, foster engagement, and align with the platform's dynamic nature. Here are some content strategies to enhance your TikTok presence:

1. Understand Your Audience:

- Analyze your audience's demographics, interests, and preferences.
   - Tailor your content to cater to your target audience's tastes.

2. Follow Trends and Challenges:
   - Participate in popular trends and challenges to increase visibility.
   - Use trending sounds, hashtags, and formats relevant to your niche.

3. Create Original Content:
   - Showcase your creativity by producing unique and original content.
   - Develop a signature style or theme that sets your content apart.

4. Use Captivating Thumbnails:
   - Craft eye-catching thumbnails to encourage clicks and views.
   - Thumbnails should provide a sneak peek into the content's excitement.

5. Engage Quickly:
   - Capture attention within the first few seconds of your video.
   - Use a hook, interesting visuals, or a compelling question to grab viewers' interest.

6. Short and Sweet:
   - Keep videos concise and within TikTok's time limit (15 to 60 seconds).
   - Prioritize delivering a clear message or entertainment quickly.

7. Tell a Story:
   - Narratives and storytelling captivate audiences.
   - Create a beginning, middle, and end structure to keep viewers engaged.

8. Utilize TikTok Features:
   - Take advantage of features like duets, stitches, and live streaming.
   - Experiment with creative effects, filters, and interactive elements.

9. Encourage Engagement:
   - Pose questions, ask for opinions, or create polls to encourage interaction.
   - Respond to comments and engage with your audience in a genuine manner.

10. Consistent Posting Schedule:
   - Establish a consistent posting schedule to keep your audience engaged.

- Regular posting increases visibility and improves your chances of appearing on the For You Page.

11. Cross-Promote on Other Platforms:
   - Share your TikTok content on other social media platforms to increase reach.
   - Utilize your existing audience on other platforms to drive traffic to your TikTok account.

12. Collaborate with Other Creators:
   - Collaborate with fellow TikTok creators to reach new audiences.
   - Duets and collaboration videos often generate increased engagement.

13. Educational Content:
   - Share useful tips, tutorials, or educational content related to your niche.
   - Position yourself as an authority in your field.

14. Utilize Trends Strategically:
   - Jump on trending challenges but add your unique twist to stand out.
   - Monitor evolving trends and adapt your content accordingly.

15. Track Analytics:
   - Use TikTok Analytics to assess the performance of your content.
   - Understand what works well and adjust your strategy based on insights.

16. Embrace Virality:
   - While not guaranteed, creating shareable and relatable content increases the chances of going viral.
   - Monitor trends and capitalize on emerging opportunities.

Remember that TikTok's algorithm rewards creativity, consistency, and engagement. By incorporating these strategies into your content creation process, you can enhance your chances of success and build a loyal and enthusiastic TikTok following.

Growing Your Audience

Leveraging Hashtags for Visibility

Leveraging hashtags effectively on TikTok is crucial for increasing the visibility of your content and reaching a wider audience. Here are some tips on how to use hashtags strategically:

1. Use Relevant Hashtags:
   - Choose hashtags that directly relate to the content of your video.

- Use a mix of popular and niche-specific hashtags to maximize visibility.

2. Explore Trending Hashtags:
   - Regularly check TikTok's Discover page to identify trending hashtags.
   - Participate in challenges or trends associated with popular hashtags to increase your chances of getting featured.

3. Create Your Own Branded Hashtag:
   - Develop a unique and memorable branded hashtag for your content.
   - Encourage your audience to use your hashtag when recreating or engaging with your content.

4. Limit the Number of Hashtags:
   - While TikTok allows up to 100 characters for captions, avoid overwhelming your caption with too many hashtags.
   - Aim for a balance between visibility and a clean, engaging caption.

5. Mix Broad and Specific Hashtags:
   - Use a combination of broad, general hashtags and more specific, niche hashtags.
   - Broad hashtags increase your content's discoverability, while niche hashtags target a specific audience.

6. Research Popular Hashtags in Your Niche:
   - Identify popular hashtags within your content's niche.
   - Incorporate these hashtags to tap into existing communities and trends.

7. Create a Hashtag Strategy:
   - Develop a hashtag strategy for your content, ensuring consistency across videos.
   - Align your hashtags with your brand, niche, and the type of content you produce.

8. **Use Hashtags in Captions or Comments:
   - Place hashtags in your video captions or the comments section to maintain a clean caption.
   - Experiment with both approaches to see what works best for your content.

9. Monitor Hashtag Performance:
   - Regularly check the performance of videos associated with specific hashtags.

- Identify which hashtags result in higher engagement and consider using them more frequently.

10. **Encourage User Participation:
   - Prompt your audience to use specific hashtags in their own content.
   - This can create a sense of community and increase the reach of your hashtag.

11. Stay Aware of Popular Challenges:
   - Participate in or create content around popular challenges with associated hashtags.
   - Riding on the momentum of trending challenges can boost your video's visibility.

12. Experiment with Branded Hashtag Campaigns:
   - If applicable, run branded hashtag campaigns to encourage user-generated content.
   - Promote these campaigns across your social media channels to reach a broader audience.

13. Be Mindful of Seasonal Hashtags:
   - Incorporate seasonal or event-specific hashtags into your content.
   - This can capitalize on trending topics and keep your content relevant.

14. Optimize Hashtags for Searchability:
   - Choose hashtags that are likely to be searched by users interested in your content.
   - Think about how potential viewers might discover your videos through search.

By incorporating these hashtag strategies into your TikTok content, you can increase the discoverability of your videos, engage with a broader audience, and potentially enhance your chances of appearing on the For You Page.

Collaborations and Duets

Collaborations and duets are powerful features on TikTok that can help you expand your reach, connect with other creators, and engage with a broader audience. Here are tips on leveraging collaborations and duets effectively:

   Collaborations:

1. Find Compatible Creators:

- Identify creators whose content complements yours or aligns with your niche.
- Look for users with a similar follower count to ensure a mutually beneficial collaboration.

2. Engage Before Collaborating:
- Interact with potential collaborators by liking, commenting, and sharing their content.
- Building a rapport beforehand increases the likelihood of a successful collaboration.

3. Reach Out Professionally:
- Send a direct message proposing the collaboration.
- Clearly outline your idea, including the type of content, theme, or challenge you have in mind.

4. Discuss Collaboration Details:
- Coordinate on the concept, format, and timeline for the collaboration.
- Clarify any specific requirements or guidelines for the content.

5. Promote Each Other:
- Cross-promote the collaboration on your respective TikTok accounts.
- Encourage your followers to check out your collaborator's content and vice versa.

6. Tag and Mention:
- Tag and mention your collaborator in the caption or comments.
- This helps in mutual visibility and makes it easier for viewers to discover both creators.

7. Encourage Engagement:
- Prompt your followers to engage with the collaboration by liking, commenting, and sharing.
- Engaging content is more likely to be featured on the For You Page.

Duets:

1. Choose the Right Video:
- Select a video from a creator you admire or one that complements your style.
- Duets work well when the content naturally lends itself to collaboration.

2. Create Engaging Thumbnails:

- Craft a compelling thumbnail to entice users to watch the duet.
- Thumbnails are crucial for capturing attention and encouraging clicks.

3. Add Your Unique Spin:
- Put your creative twist on the duet to make it unique.
- Whether it's adding commentary, reacting, or enhancing the content, make it your own.

4. Engage in a Conversation:
- Use the duet feature to engage in a virtual conversation with another creator.
- React to their content or respond to their message in a creative way.

5. Encourage Duets from Your Followers:
- Create content that invites your followers to duet with you.
- This fosters a sense of community and can lead to a variety of creative collaborations.

6. Experiment with Trending Duets:
- Participate in trending duets or challenges on the Discover page.
- This increases the likelihood of your duet being seen by a wider audience.

7. Collaborate with Your Audience:
- Duet with your followers' content to show appreciation and foster a sense of community.
- This creates a more interactive and engaging experience for your audience.

8. Acknowledge Duets in Your Content:
- Acknowledge and appreciate duets in your subsequent videos.
- This encourages more users to engage with your content through duets.

Remember, both collaborations and duets should align with your brand and the type of content you want to be associated with. By leveraging these features strategically, you can enhance your visibility, foster community engagement, and create dynamic content that resonates with a wider audience on TikTok.

Engaging with Your Audience

Engaging with your audience is crucial for building a strong and loyal community on TikTok. Here are effective strategies to foster interaction and connection with your audience:

1. Respond to Comments:

- Regularly check and respond to comments on your videos.
- Engage with your audience by answering questions, expressing gratitude, or starting conversations.

2. Ask Questions:
- Pose questions in your videos or captions to encourage viewer participation.
- Create content that invites your audience to share their opinions and experiences.

3. Host Q&A Sessions:
- Occasionally host Q&A sessions where followers can ask you questions.
- Respond to questions in subsequent videos or dedicate a specific video to answering queries.

4. Encourage User-Generated Content (UGC):
- Prompt your followers to create content related to your niche or participate in challenges.
- Highlight and react to UGC in your videos, showing appreciation for your community's creativity.

5. Use Polls and Challenges:
- Utilize TikTok's interactive features, such as polls and challenges.
- Polls are a quick way to gather opinions, while challenges encourage user participation.

6. Engage in Duets:
- Participate in duets with your followers' videos.
- This creates a collaborative and inclusive atmosphere, showcasing your appreciation for your audience.

7. Host Live Streams:
- Go live to interact with your audience in real-time.
- Respond to comments, answer questions, and acknowledge viewers during your live sessions.

8. Show Behind-the-Scenes:
- Share behind-the-scenes glimpses of your life or content creation process.
- This adds a personal touch and allows your audience to connect with you on a more authentic level.

9. Acknowledge and Celebrate Milestones:
- Celebrate follower milestones by creating special content or thanking your audience.

- Acknowledge your community's support and express your gratitude.

10. Run Contests and Giveaways:
   - Host contests or giveaways to encourage engagement.
   - Ask followers to participate by creating content, sharing your videos, or commenting to enter.

11. Feature Fan Shoutouts:
   - Feature shoutouts for your followers in your videos or captions.
   - This recognition makes your audience feel valued and appreciated.

12. Create Diverse Content:
   - Offer a variety of content to cater to different interests within your audience.
   - Gauge reactions and adjust your content strategy based on what resonates most with your viewers.

13. Monitor Analytics:
   - Use TikTok Analytics to understand which videos perform well and why.
   - Tailor your future content based on the preferences of your audience.

14. Promote Community Guidelines:
   - Establish community guidelines to foster a positive and respectful environment.
   - Address any negativity promptly and encourage a supportive community.

15. Stay Consistent:
   - Maintain a consistent posting schedule to keep your audience engaged.
   - Consistency builds anticipation and helps you stay connected with your followers.

By actively engaging with your audience, you create a sense of community, strengthen your brand, and encourage long-term loyalty. Pay attention to your audience's feedback, adapt your content based on their preferences, and make them feel like valued participants in your TikTok journey.

Monetization Strategies

TikTok Creator Fund

Here are the key aspects of the TikTok Creator Fund based on the information available up to my last update:

1. Eligibility Criteria:
   - Creators need to meet specific eligibility requirements to participate in the Creator Fund.
   - These criteria typically include factors such as age, follower count, and compliance with TikTok's community guidelines.

2. Funding Opportunities:
   - Once accepted into the Creator Fund, eligible creators can access financial support directly from TikTok.
   - The fund aims to reward creators for their contributions to the platform and encourage them to continue producing high-quality content.

3. Payment Structure:
   - The payment structure within the Creator Fund can vary.
   - Creators may receive payments based on a variety of factors, including the engagement their content receives, the number of followers they have, and other performance metrics.

4. Exclusive Features and Support:
   - In addition to financial support, creators in the fund may gain access to exclusive features, tools, or resources to enhance their content creation experience on TikTok.

5. Content Requirements:
   - Creators are often required to produce content that aligns with TikTok's community standards and guidelines.
   - Adhering to TikTok's content policies is crucial to remain eligible for the Creator Fund.

6. Application Process:
   - Creators interested in joining the Creator Fund typically need to apply through the TikTok app.
   - The application process may involve submitting details about their account, content, and audience.

7. Global Availability:
   - The TikTok Creator Fund has expanded to various countries to support creators worldwide.
   - Eligibility and payment structures may vary based on regional considerations.

It's important to note that the TikTok platform and its features, including the Creator Fund, may have evolved since my last update.

Creators interested in joining the TikTok Creator Fund or learning about any changes to the program should refer to the latest information provided by TikTok through its official channels or support documentation.

Live Gifts and Donations

Here are the key aspects of live gifts and donations on TikTok:

1. Virtual Gifts:

- Viewers can purchase virtual gifts using in-app currency, which is often referred to as "coins" on TikTok.

- These virtual gifts can include various animated stickers, emojis, or other graphical elements that appear on the screen during the live stream.

2. Monetary Donations:

- In addition to virtual gifts, TikTok may allow users to make monetary donations directly to creators during live streams.

- Creators may receive a share of the donation amount as a way of monetizing their live content.

3. Gift Points and Diamond Gifts:

- TikTok often assigns point values to virtual gifts, and creators can accumulate these points during their live streams.

- The collected points may contribute to a creator's overall status, and users may aim to send higher-value gifts, such as diamond gifts, for increased visibility and recognition.

4. Gift Leaderboard:

- TikTok usually displays a gift leaderboard during live streams, showcasing the users who have sent the most gifts or contributed the highest total value.

- This leaderboard can create a competitive and interactive element during live broadcasts.

5. Cash Out and Earnings:

- Creators typically have the option to cash out or withdraw their earnings from virtual gifts and donations.

- The process and requirements for cashing out may vary based on TikTok's policies and the creator's location.

6. Fan Support:

- Live gifts and donations provide a way for fans to show their appreciation and support for their favorite creators in real-time.

- It establishes a direct connection between creators and their audience, allowing fans to contribute to the success of the creators they enjoy.

Creators interested in utilizing the live gifts and donations feature should review TikTok's official guidelines and documentation to understand the platform's policies, eligibility criteria, and any recent updates to the monetization features. TikTok may introduce new features or modify existing ones to enhance the creator experience and further support the platform's ecosystem.

Sponsored Content and Brand Deals

Sponsored content and brand deals are popular ways for TikTok creators to monetize their influence and collaborations with businesses. If you're a content creator looking to work with brands on TikTok, here are some key considerations:

1. Build a Strong Profile:
   - Before attracting brand partnerships, build a strong and authentic TikTok profile with engaging content.
   - Focus on growing your follower base and engagement metrics.

2. Identify Your Niche and Audience:
   - Clearly define your niche and understand your target audience.
   - Brands are more likely to collaborate with creators whose content aligns with their target demographic.

3. Engage with Your Audience:
   - Cultivate an engaged and interactive community on TikTok.
   - Brands often seek creators with an active and responsive audience.

4. Create a Media Kit:
   - Develop a media kit that showcases your TikTok profile, audience demographics, engagement metrics, and past collaborations.
   - Include information about your content style, interests, and the value you can offer to potential partners.

5. Contact Brands Directly:
   - Reach out to brands you admire or that align with your niche.
   - Craft professional and personalized pitches, emphasizing the value you can bring to their marketing efforts.

6. Join Influencer Marketing Platforms:
   - Explore influencer marketing platforms that connect creators with brands looking for collaborations.

- Platforms like Tribe, Influencity, or AspireIQ may facilitate partnerships.

7. Disclose Partnerships Transparently:
- Clearly disclose sponsored content to maintain transparency with your audience.
- TikTok also encourages creators to use the #ad or #sponsored hashtags to indicate promotional content.

8. Negotiate Fair Compensation:
- Understand your worth and negotiate fair compensation for your work.
- Consider factors such as the scope of the collaboration, deliverables, and the time and effort involved.

9. Collaborate with Brands You Believe In:
- Prioritize collaborations with brands whose products or services you genuinely support.
- Authenticity is key to maintaining trust with your audience.

10. Deliver High-Quality Content:
- Create content that aligns with both your style and the brand's messaging.
- Ensure that the sponsored content is seamlessly integrated into your usual content.

11. Understand Brand Objectives:
- Communicate with the brand to understand their goals and objectives for the collaboration.
- Tailor your content to meet the brand's expectations and resonate with their target audience.

12. Measure and Report Performance:
- Provide brands with insights and analytics on the performance of sponsored content.
- Be transparent about engagement metrics, reach, and other relevant data.

13. Negotiate Long-Term Partnerships:
- Establish long-term partnerships with brands when possible.
- Consistent collaborations with the same brands can contribute to a stable income stream.

14. Stay Compliant with TikTok Policies:
- Familiarize yourself with TikTok's advertising policies and guidelines.
- Adhere to the platform's rules to avoid any potential issues.

Remember that successful collaborations benefit both the creator and the brand. By approaching partnerships professionally, delivering high-quality content, and maintaining authenticity, you can create valuable and lasting relationships with brands on TikTok.

Selling Merchandise on TikTok

-
- Here's a general overview of how selling merchandise on TikTok works:

-
-

- **1. Merch Shelf:**
- - TikTok provides a Merch Shelf feature that allows eligible creators to showcase and sell their branded merchandise directly on their profile.
- - This shelf appears on the creator's TikTok profile and can be customized to display various products.

-
- **2. Integration with Merch Partners:**
- - TikTok has partnered with various third-party merchandise providers to facilitate the creation, production, and fulfillment of merchandise.
- - Creators can choose from these partners to design and offer a variety of products to their audience.

-
- **3. Eligibility Criteria:**
- - Not all creators may have immediate access to the Merch Shelf feature.
- - TikTok typically extends this feature to creators who meet certain eligibility criteria, such as having a certain follower count and adhering to community guidelines.

-
- **4. Setting Up the Merch Shelf:**
- - Creators can set up their Merch Shelf through the TikTok app, where they link to their merchandise store and customize the appearance of the shelf.
- - The shelf may include product images, prices, and links to the external merchandise store.

-

Unlocking the Power of Affiliate Marketing

Unlocking the power of affiliate marketing on TikTok can be a lucrative way to monetize your content while promoting products or services that align with your niche. Here are steps and strategies to make the most of affiliate marketing on TikTok:

1. Choose Relevant Affiliate Programs:

- Select affiliate programs that align with your content and resonate with your audience. Look for products or services that you genuinely believe in and that your followers would find valuable.

2. Disclose Your Affiliation:

- Be transparent with your audience about your affiliate partnerships. Clearly disclose when you are promoting products or services for which you may earn a commission.

3. Create Compelling Content:

- Develop engaging and authentic content around the affiliate products. Showcase how the products or services solve a problem, meet a need, or enhance the lives of your followers.

4. Tell a Story:

- Incorporate storytelling into your content to make it more relatable. Share personal experiences, demonstrate product use, or highlight how the affiliate offering fits into your daily life.

5. Use TikTok Features Creatively:

- Leverage TikTok's features such as duets, stitches, and creative effects to make your affiliate marketing content stand out. Interactive and visually appealing content tends to capture more attention.

6. Feature Call-to-Action (CTA):

- Include a clear call-to-action in your videos, encouraging viewers to click on the affiliate link or use a specific code to make a purchase. Consider adding the CTA in both the video and caption.

7. Utilize Swipe-Up Links:

- If you have access to the TikTok Creator Fund or TikTok Live Gifts and are eligible for the "swipe-up" feature, use it to direct your audience to the affiliate link or landing page directly.

8. Host Live Q&A Sessions:

- Consider hosting live Q&A sessions to answer questions about the affiliate products. Live interactions can build trust and provide real-time information to your audience.

9. Offer Exclusive Deals:

- Negotiate with the affiliate program to provide exclusive discounts or deals for your followers. Exclusive offerings can incentivize your audience to make a purchase through your affiliate link.

10. Track Performance:

- Monitor the performance of your affiliate marketing campaigns. Track clicks, conversions, and other relevant metrics to understand what works best for your audience.

11. Optimize Timing:

- Consider the timing of your affiliate marketing content. Promote products during relevant seasons, holidays, or events when your audience may be more inclined to make purchases.

12. Diversify Affiliate Partnerships:

- Diversify your affiliate partnerships to include a range of products or services. This can prevent your content from becoming too promotional and offer variety to your audience.

13. Engage with Your Audience:

- Engage with your audience by responding to comments, asking for feedback, and incorporating their suggestions into your content. Building a community fosters trust and strengthens your influence.

14. Stay Compliant with Guidelines:

- Adhere to TikTok's community guidelines and advertising policies when creating affiliate marketing content. Ensuring compliance helps maintain a positive relationship with the platform and your audience.

Remember to continuously assess the effectiveness of your affiliate marketing efforts and adjust your strategy based on the feedback and preferences of your TikTok audience. By combining authenticity, creativity, and strategic promotion, you can unlock the full potential of affiliate marketing on TikTok.

Legal Considerations

Copyright and Music Usage

Copyright and music usage are critical legal considerations when creating content on platforms like TikTok. TikTok, like other social media platforms, has guidelines and policies to ensure that users respect copyright laws. Here are some key legal considerations related to copyright and music usage on TikTok:

1. Licensed Music:

- Use only music that you have the right to use. TikTok provides a vast library of licensed music that users can incorporate into their videos without worrying about copyright issues.

2. Original Content:

- Create and use original music or content to avoid copyright infringement. If you compose your music or use royalty-free tracks, you have more control over the usage rights.

3. TikTok's Music Library:

- TikTok has a built-in music library with a wide range of songs that users can use freely in their content. Explore this library to find tracks that suit your videos without violating copyright.

4. License and Permission:

- If you want to use a specific song that is not available in TikTok's library, ensure you have the necessary license or permission from the copyright holder. This might involve reaching out to the artist, label, or licensing agency.

5. Public Domain Music:

- Use music that is in the public domain, as it is not subject to copyright restrictions. However, ensure that the specific recording or performance is also in the public domain.

6. Fair Use Consideration:

- Understand the concept of fair use, but be cautious. Fair use is a legal doctrine that allows the use of copyrighted material under certain circumstances. However, it's a complex legal concept, and misinterpretation can lead to legal issues.

7. Avoid Unauthorized Reproduction:

- Do not reproduce or upload music tracks that you do not have the right to use. Unauthorized reproduction can lead to copyright claims, and TikTok may take down content that violates copyright policies.

8. Attribution and Credit:

- If you use music that requires attribution, ensure that you give proper credit to the artist or copyright holder in your video description or caption.

9. Transformative Content:

- Create content that transforms the original work, adding new value or meaning. Transformative content may have stronger arguments for fair use, but it's not a guaranteed defense.

10. DMCA Compliance:

- TikTok complies with the Digital Millennium Copyright Act (DMCA). If your content receives a copyright claim, TikTok may take it down, and repeated violations could lead to account suspension.

11. Educate Yourself:

- Familiarize yourself with TikTok's community guidelines, terms of service, and copyright policies. Staying informed about platform rules will help you create content within the legal boundaries.

12. Use TikTok's Tools:

- TikTok provides tools for users to select and use licensed music easily. Utilize these tools to stay within the platform's copyright guidelines.

Remember that laws and platform policies may change over time, so it's essential to stay informed about the latest updates. Always respect intellectual property rights and create content that complies with copyright laws to ensure a positive and legal experience on TikTok. If you have specific legal concerns, consider consulting with a legal professional familiar with intellectual property and social media laws.

Disclosures and Transparency

Disclosures and transparency are crucial elements when creating content on TikTok or any other social media platform. Being clear and open with your audience helps build trust and ensures compliance with legal and ethical standards. Here are key considerations for disclosures and transparency on TikTok:

1. Affiliate Marketing and Sponsored Content:

- Clearly disclose any affiliations, partnerships, or sponsorships in your content. Use captions, hashtags, or verbal statements to inform your audience when you are promoting products or services for which you may earn a commission.

2. Use Disclosures in Captions:

- Include relevant disclosures in your video captions, especially when promoting or endorsing products. Be explicit about any commercial relationships or benefits you may receive.

3. #Ad and #Sponsored:

- Use hashtags like #Ad or #Sponsored to signal that your content is part of a paid partnership or includes sponsored elements. TikTok's algorithm recognizes these tags and may provide additional visibility for transparent content.

4. Branded Content Tools:
   - If using TikTok's branded content tools, make use of the "Paid Promotion" feature. This feature allows you to disclose your partnership directly within the platform.

5. Educate Your Audience:
   - Educate your audience about the nature of brand deals and sponsorships. Explain what it means when you use certain hashtags or disclose partnerships to foster transparency and understanding.

6. Full Disclosure in Product Reviews:
   - When reviewing products, especially if they were provided for free or as part of a collaboration, clearly disclose the nature of the relationship. Your audience has the right to know if you received products or compensation.

7. Authenticity Matters:
   - Be authentic and genuine in your disclosures. Avoid misleading or unclear statements that could confuse your audience about the nature of your relationships with brands or products.

8. Transparency in Challenges and Giveaways:
   - If conducting challenges or giveaways that involve partnerships or sponsorships, disclose this information. Be transparent about the terms and conditions of the challenge or giveaway.

9. Adhere to TikTok's Policies:
   - Familiarize yourself with TikTok's community guidelines and advertising policies. Ensure that your content aligns with the platform's rules regarding transparency and disclosure.

10. Update Your Bio:
   - Consider updating your TikTok bio to include a brief note about collaborations or partnerships. This serves as a constant reminder to your audience about your approach to sponsored content.

11. Honesty in Reviews:
   - If providing reviews, opinions, or testimonials, maintain honesty and transparency. Clearly state whether you received compensation or products in exchange for your review.

12. Legal Compliance:
   - Adhere to relevant laws and regulations governing influencer marketing and content creation in your jurisdiction. Compliance with legal standards is essential for maintaining trust and avoiding legal issues.

Remember that transparency is not only a legal requirement but also a key factor in building a loyal and engaged audience. By being open about your collaborations and partnerships, you contribute to a positive online community and reinforce trust with your followers.

Protecting Your Intellectual Property

Protecting your intellectual property is essential when creating content on TikTok or any other platform. Intellectual property includes your original creations, such as videos, music, designs, and any unique content you produce. Here are steps to help safeguard your intellectual property on TikTok:

1. Understand TikTok's Terms of Service:

- Familiarize yourself with TikTok's terms of service and community guidelines. Knowing the platform's rules will help you navigate potential intellectual property issues.

2. Use Original Content:

- Create and use original content to reduce the risk of infringing on someone else's intellectual property. Original content is also more likely to be protected under copyright law.

3. Respect Copyrighted Material:

- Avoid using copyrighted material, such as music, images, or videos, without permission. TikTok has a library of licensed music that you can use freely, but using external copyrighted material may lead to copyright claims.

4. Obtain Proper Licensing:

- If you plan to use music or any other content that you don't own, obtain the necessary licenses or permissions. This is particularly important for commercial use or monetization.

5. Watermark Your Content:

- Consider adding a watermark to your videos. While this doesn't provide legal protection, it serves as a visible indicator of ownership and discourages unauthorized use.

6. Register Your Copyright:

- In some jurisdictions, registering your original content with the appropriate copyright office can provide additional legal protection. Check the copyright laws in your country for guidance.

7. Utilize TikTok's Tools:

- TikTok offers tools to help creators protect their content. For instance, you can enable settings to prevent others from downloading your videos or duetting with them.

8. Monitor and Report Violations:
   - Regularly monitor your content and be vigilant for potential violations. If you discover unauthorized use of your intellectual property, report it to TikTok through the platform's reporting mechanisms.
9. Trademark Protection:
   - If you have a unique brand or logo associated with your content, consider seeking trademark protection. This can provide legal recourse if others attempt to use similar marks.
10. Terms in Contracts:
   - If you collaborate with others, such as music producers, ensure that your agreements clearly outline the ownership and usage rights of the intellectual property involved.
11. Educate Your Audience:
   - Educate your audience about intellectual property rights and the importance of respecting creators' work. This can foster a community that values and respects original content.
12. Consult Legal Professionals:
   - If you have concerns about protecting your intellectual property, consider consulting with legal professionals specializing in intellectual property law. They can provide tailored advice based on your specific situation.
Remember that protecting intellectual property is an ongoing process, and staying informed about legal standards and platform policies is crucial. By taking proactive steps and being vigilant, you can help safeguard your creative work on TikTok and other platforms.

Advanced TikTok Tactics

Utilizing TikTok Ads

Utilizing TikTok Ads can be a powerful strategy to expand your reach, engage with a larger audience, and achieve specific marketing goals. TikTok offers various ad formats and targeting options to suit different business objectives. Here are advanced tactics for effectively using TikTok Ads:

1. Understand Ad Formats:
   - Familiarize yourself with TikTok's ad formats, including In-Feed Ads, Branded Hashtag Challenges, Branded Effects, TopView Ads, and Branded Scan. Each format has its unique features and use cases.

2. Set Clear Objectives:
- Define clear marketing objectives before creating TikTok Ads. Whether it's increasing brand awareness, driving app installations, or promoting a specific product, having a clear goal will guide your ad strategy.

3. Utilize TikTok Pixel:
- Implement the TikTok Pixel on your website to track user interactions and gather valuable data for optimization. The Pixel helps you measure the effectiveness of your ads and enables retargeting for better conversions.

4. Experiment with Custom Audiences:
- Leverage TikTok's Custom Audiences feature to target specific groups based on their previous interactions with your brand, website visits, or engagement with your TikTok content.

5. Lookalike Audiences:
- Create Lookalike Audiences to target users who share similar characteristics and behaviors with your existing customer base. This helps in reaching a new audience that is likely to be interested in your offerings.

6. Optimize Ad Placements:
- Test different ad placements within the TikTok app to see which performs best for your goals. Experiment with In-Feed Ads, Explore Page Ads, and other placements to find the most effective option.

7. Engage with Hashtag Challenges:
- Participate in or create Branded Hashtag Challenges to encourage user-generated content. This fosters engagement and user participation, extending the reach of your brand organically.

8. Collaborate with Influencers:
- Partner with TikTok influencers to amplify your ad campaigns. Influencers can provide authentic endorsements and help your brand connect with their followers on a more personal level.

9. Use Interactive Elements:
- Incorporate interactive elements into your ads, such as polling, quiz questions, or call-to-action buttons. This enhances user engagement and encourages users to take immediate action.

10. Optimize Ad Creative:
- Invest time in creating visually appealing and engaging ad creatives. Use TikTok's creative tools, filters, and effects to make

your ads stand out and align with the platform's dynamic and creative nature.

11. Implement Bid Strategies:
   - Experiment with different bid strategies, such as Maximum Bid, Target Cost, or Minimum ROAS (Return on Ad Spend). Monitor performance metrics and adjust your bid strategy based on the results.

12. Dayparting and Scheduling:
   - Use dayparting to schedule your ads during specific times of the day when your target audience is most active. Experiment with different schedules to optimize ad delivery.

13. A/B Testing:
   - Conduct A/B testing with different ad creatives, copy, and targeting options. Analyze the performance of each variant to identify what resonates best with your audience and refine your strategy accordingly.

14. Optimize Landing Pages:
   - Ensure that the landing pages linked to your TikTok Ads are optimized for mobile devices and provide a seamless user experience. A well-optimized landing page contributes to better conversion rates.

15. Monitor Analytics and Adjust:
   - Regularly review TikTok Analytics to assess the performance of your ads. Track key metrics, such as impressions, click-through rates, and conversion rates. Make data-driven adjustments to optimize your campaigns.

By implementing these advanced tactics, you can elevate your TikTok Ads strategy and maximize the impact of your advertising efforts on the platform. Experimentation, data analysis, and ongoing optimization are key components of a successful TikTok Ads campaign.

Going Viral: Strategies for Success

Going viral on TikTok involves a combination of creativity, timing, and understanding the platform's dynamics. While there's no guaranteed formula for virality, certain strategies can increase your chances of creating content that resonates with a large audience. Here are some strategies for success:

1. Understand TikTok Trends:

- Stay informed about the latest trends, challenges, and hashtags on TikTok. Participating in popular trends can give your content visibility and increase the likelihood of reaching a broader audience.

2. Original and Creative Content:

- Create content that stands out by bringing a unique and creative perspective. TikTok users appreciate originality, humor, and authenticity. Find ways to put your creative spin on popular trends or create entirely new concepts.

3. Engage Quickly:

- TikTok's algorithm values engagement, especially during the initial moments of a video being posted. Respond to comments promptly, and encourage viewers to like, share, and engage with your content.

4. Leverage TikTok Challenges:

- Participate in or create your own TikTok challenges. Challenges often gain momentum quickly, and users enjoy participating in them. Be sure to use relevant hashtags to maximize discoverability.

5. Create Shareable Content:

- Craft content that viewers want to share with their friends. Whether it's funny, heartwarming, or surprising, shareable content is more likely to be distributed widely on TikTok.

6. Utilize Hashtags Effectively:

- Use trending and relevant hashtags to increase the discoverability of your content. Research popular hashtags within your niche and incorporate them into your captions to tap into existing communities.

7. Optimize Thumbnail and Captions:

- Design an eye-catching thumbnail that encourages users to click on your video. Craft compelling captions that provide context, intrigue, or a call-to-action. A well-crafted caption can entice users to watch and share your content.

8. Timing Matters:

- Pay attention to when you post your content. Consider the peak times when your target audience is most active on TikTok. Posting during these times can increase your video's visibility.

9. Engage with Trends Quickly:

- Be quick to jump on emerging trends. The faster you engage with a trend, the higher the chance of your content being seen and featured on the For You Page.

10. Collaborate with Other Creators:

- Collaborate with other TikTok creators to leverage their audience and increase the reach of your content. Duets and collaborations often result in mutual exposure to both creators' followers.

11. Create Content for the For You Page:

- Aim to create content that appeals to a broad audience. TikTok's For You Page (FYP) algorithm promotes content based on user interests, so crafting content with wide appeal can increase your chances of landing on the FYP.

12. Consistent Posting Schedule:

- Maintain a consistent posting schedule to keep your audience engaged. Regularly sharing content increases your visibility on the platform and encourages viewers to follow you.

13. Spark Emotions:

- Content that evokes strong emotions—joy, surprise, laughter, or empathy—tends to perform well on TikTok. Connect with your audience emotionally to leave a lasting impression.

14. Optimize Video Length:

- Keep your videos concise and engaging. While TikTok allows longer videos, shorter, punchy content often performs better. Capture attention quickly and maintain viewer interest throughout the video.

15. Promote on Other Platforms:

- Share your TikTok videos on other social media platforms to cross-promote and drive additional traffic to your TikTok account. Utilize your existing audience on other platforms to boost your TikTok visibility.

Remember that TikTok's algorithm is dynamic, and there's an element of unpredictability in virality. Keep experimenting, analyzing performance metrics, and adapting your strategy based on audience feedback to increase your chances of creating content that goes viral.

Trends and Challenges: Riding the Wave

Riding the wave of TikTok trends and challenges can significantly boost your visibility and engagement on the platform. Staying current with the latest trends and actively participating in challenges allows you to tap into the collective creativity of the TikTok community. Here are strategies for effectively riding the wave of TikTok trends and challenges:

1. Stay Informed:

- Regularly explore the Discover page and follow trending hashtags to stay informed about the latest challenges and trends. Being aware of what's popular helps you integrate relevant content into your strategy.

2. Act Quickly:

- TikTok trends can emerge and fade quickly. Act promptly by creating content that aligns with or puts a unique spin on current trends. Early participation increases the visibility of your videos on the For You Page.

3. Put Your Spin on Trends:

- While it's essential to follow trends, adding your creative twist sets your content apart. Personalize the trend or challenge to showcase your unique style, humor, or perspective.

4. Consistent Theme:

- Maintain a consistent theme or aesthetic in your content while participating in trends. This helps build a recognizable brand identity that stands out even when engaging with popular challenges.

5. Create Original Challenges:

- Develop your challenges or trends to encourage user participation. Original challenges have the potential to go viral, and your brand can become synonymous with a specific trend.

6. Engage with Challenges Authentically:

- Engage with challenges authentically, ensuring that your participation feels natural and aligns with your brand voice. Authenticity resonates with TikTok users and enhances your content's appeal.

7. Leverage Duets and Stitches:

- Participate in duets or stitches related to trending challenges. This interactive form of content creation allows you to engage with other users, expanding your reach within the TikTok community.

8. Interact with the Community:

- Respond to comments, engage with other creators participating in the same challenge, and foster a sense of community. Building connections enhances your visibility and encourages others to engage with your content.

9. Explore Niche Trends:

- While global trends are valuable, also explore niche trends within your specific content niche. Participating in niche trends can help you connect with a more targeted audience interested in your content.

10. Adapt to Different Niches:

- Be flexible and adapt your content to different niches or categories of trends. This versatility allows you to appeal to a broader audience and increase the discoverability of your content.

11. Create How-To Content:

- If a challenge involves a specific skill or activity, create how-to content to guide others. Providing valuable information and tips can enhance your authority within the TikTok community.

12. Monitor Analytics:

- Track the performance of your trend-related content using TikTok Analytics. Analyze engagement metrics, views, and follower growth to understand the impact of your participation in trends.

13. Collaborate with Other Creators:

- Collaborate with other TikTok creators participating in the same trend. Duets, collaborations, and shoutouts can introduce your content to new audiences and amplify your reach.

14. Incorporate Trending Sounds:

- Pay attention to trending sounds on TikTok and incorporate them into your content. Using popular sounds can enhance the discoverability of your videos and make them more relatable to viewers.

15. Stay Positive and Fun:

- Most TikTok trends and challenges thrive on positivity and fun. Keep your content lighthearted, and showcase your personality to create an enjoyable viewing experience for your audience.

By actively participating in TikTok trends and challenges, you can enhance your content's visibility, connect with a broader audience, and foster community engagement. Be creative, stay informed, and infuse your unique style into trend participation to make the most of this dynamic and rapidly evolving platform.

Diversifying Your Revenue Streams

Cross-Platform Promotion

Cross-platform promotion is a powerful strategy for expanding your online presence and reaching a broader audience. Here are effective ways to promote your TikTok content across multiple platforms:

1. Share TikTok Videos on Other Social Media:

- Cross-promote your TikTok content by sharing your videos on platforms like Instagram, Twitter, Facebook, and Snapchat. Use the native sharing features within the TikTok app to post your videos on other social networks.

2. Create Teasers for Other Platforms:

- Build anticipation by creating teaser content for your TikTok videos and sharing them on other platforms. Teasers can include snippets or highlights to pique the interest of your audience and encourage them to check out the full video on TikTok.

3. Utilize Instagram Stories and Reels:

- Share short clips or screenshots of your TikTok videos on Instagram Stories. Additionally, you can create content specifically for Instagram Reels, utilizing the platform's short-form video format to showcase your TikTok content.

4. Twitter Highlights:

- Tweet highlights or interesting moments from your TikTok videos on Twitter. Use relevant hashtags and captions to grab the attention of your Twitter audience and drive them to your TikTok profile.

5. LinkedIn Sharing:

- Share educational or industry-related TikTok content on LinkedIn. LinkedIn's professional audience may appreciate unique insights or tips presented in a creative format.

6. YouTube Shorts:

- Repurpose your TikTok videos for YouTube Shorts, YouTube's short-form video platform. This allows you to tap into a different audience while leveraging content you've already created.

7. Pinterest Story Pins:

- Create Story Pins on Pinterest featuring your TikTok content. This can be a visually appealing way to showcase your videos and engage with the Pinterest community.

8. Snapchat Stories:

- Share behind-the-scenes footage, snippets, or highlights from your TikTok videos on Snapchat Stories. This provides your Snapchat audience with a glimpse into your TikTok content.

9. Blog or Website Integration:

- Embed TikTok videos on your blog or website. This is especially effective if you have a blog related to your TikTok niche.

Embedding videos enhances user engagement and keeps your website visitors informed about your TikTok presence.

10. Email Newsletters:

   - Include links or embedded TikTok videos in your email newsletters. Update your subscribers about your latest TikTok content and encourage them to follow you on the platform.

11. Collaborate with Other Creators:

   - Collaborate with creators on other platforms. Cross-promote each other's content by featuring one another in videos, shoutouts, or collaborative projects.

12. Consistent Branding Across Platforms:

   - Maintain consistent branding across all platforms. Use similar profile pictures, usernames, and visual elements to create a cohesive online presence, making it easy for followers to recognize you on different platforms.

13. Promote TikTok on Your Website:

   - Add TikTok icons or widgets to your website, linking to your TikTok profile. This encourages website visitors to explore your TikTok content and follow you on the platform.

14. Engage with Cross-Promotion Groups:

   - Join cross-promotion groups or communities on social media where creators support each other by sharing content. Participating in these groups can help boost your visibility and attract new followers.

15. Host Cross-Platform Giveaways:

   - Collaborate with creators on other platforms to host cross-platform giveaways. This encourages their audience to discover your TikTok content, and vice versa.

Consistent cross-platform promotion enhances your overall online presence, attracts a diverse audience, and strengthens your brand across different channels. Tailor your promotional approach to each platform's audience and features to maximize your impact.

Creating Your Own Products

Creating your own products can be a rewarding venture, allowing you to showcase your creativity and build a brand. Whether you're interested in physical merchandise, digital products, or services, here's a step-by-step guide to help you get started:

1. Identify Your Niche:

- Determine the niche or market you want to target with your products. Understanding your audience is crucial for creating products that meet their needs and preferences.

2. Research Market Demand:

- Conduct market research to identify the demand for products within your chosen niche. Look for gaps in the market or opportunities where your unique offerings can stand out.

3. Define Your Unique Selling Proposition (USP):

- Clearly define what sets your products apart from others in the market. Your unique selling proposition should highlight the unique features, benefits, or values that make your products special.

4. Choose Product Types:

- Decide on the type of products you want to create. This could include physical goods, digital products, or services. Common product types include clothing, accessories, digital art, e-books, online courses, or consulting services.

5. Develop a Business Plan:

- Create a comprehensive business plan that outlines your goals, target market, product offerings, pricing strategy, marketing plan, and financial projections. A well-thought-out business plan serves as a roadmap for your venture.

6. Design Your Products:

- If you're creating physical goods, work on the design and prototypes. Collaborate with designers or use design tools to bring your vision to life. For digital products or services, outline the content or features you'll provide.

7. Source Suppliers or Create In-House:

- Identify suppliers or manufacturers if you're creating physical products. Consider whether you'll handle production in-house or collaborate with external partners. Ensure that your chosen suppliers align with your quality standards and values.

8. Set Up an Online Store:

- Choose a platform to sell your products, such as Shopify, Etsy, or your website. Create an online store that showcases your products effectively. Optimize product listings with high-quality images, detailed descriptions, and compelling copy.

9. Price Your Products:

- Determine the pricing strategy for your products. Consider factors such as production costs, competitors' prices, perceived value, and profit margins. Ensure that your prices align with market expectations and your brand positioning.

10. Build a Brand Identity:
   - Develop a cohesive brand identity that reflects your values and resonates with your target audience. This includes creating a memorable logo, choosing a color scheme, and defining your brand voice.

11. Implement Marketing Strategies:
   - Develop a marketing plan to promote your products. Utilize social media, influencer collaborations, content marketing, and other channels to generate awareness and drive traffic to your online store.

12. Launch Your Products:
   - Plan a launch strategy to generate excitement around your products. Consider offering exclusive deals or limited-time promotions to incentivize early purchases. Leverage social media platforms to create buzz.

13. Gather and Analyze Feedback:
   - Encourage customers to provide feedback on your products. Use this feedback to make improvements and refine your offerings. Positive reviews can also serve as valuable testimonials for future marketing.

14. Scale Your Business:
   - As your business grows, explore opportunities to scale. This may involve expanding your product line, entering new markets, or exploring additional sales channels.

15. Stay Adaptable and Innovative:
   - The business landscape is dynamic, so stay adaptable and innovative. Keep an eye on industry trends, listen to customer feedback, and be willing to evolve your products and strategies over time.

Remember that building a successful product business takes time and dedication. Stay committed to providing value to your customers, and continuously refine your approach based on market dynamics and customer feedback.

Building a Personal Brand Beyond TikTok

Building a personal brand beyond TikTok involves creating a consistent and authentic online presence across multiple platforms. Here are strategies to help you extend your personal brand beyond TikTok:

1. Define Your Brand Identity:
   - Clearly define your personal brand identity, including your values, niche, and unique selling points. Understand what sets you apart from others and what you want your audience to associate with your brand.

2. Consistent Visual Branding:
   - Maintain a consistent visual identity across platforms. Use a recognizable profile picture, consistent color schemes, and cohesive design elements in your content and on your website or blog.

3. Create a Website or Blog:
   - Establish a website or blog as a central hub for your personal brand. This platform can showcase your portfolio, provide more in-depth content, and serve as a place for your audience to learn more about you.

4. Diversify Content Platforms:
   - Extend your presence to other social media platforms, such as Instagram, YouTube, Twitter, LinkedIn, or Snapchat. Adapt your content strategy to suit the unique features and audience preferences of each platform.

5. Leverage YouTube for Long-Form Content:
   - If applicable to your content style, consider creating long-form content on YouTube. This allows you to explore topics in greater detail and provides another avenue for audience engagement.

6. Engage with Your Audience:
   - Actively engage with your audience across all platforms. Respond to comments, messages, and mentions. Building a strong connection with your audience fosters loyalty and strengthens your personal brand.

7. Collaborate with Other Creators:
   - Collaborate with creators from different platforms to expand your reach and introduce your personal brand to new audiences. Cross-platform collaborations can be mutually beneficial.

8. Participate in Industry Events:
   - Attend industry events, conferences, or meetups related to your niche. Networking with professionals in your field can enhance your credibility and broaden your personal brand's reach.

9. Guest Features and Interviews:
   - Seek opportunities to be featured as a guest on podcasts, interviews, or other creators' platforms. Sharing your insights and

experiences can elevate your authority and expose your personal brand to new audiences.

10. Create Value Through Content:
   - Focus on creating valuable and shareable content. Whether it's informative, entertaining, or inspiring, content that adds value resonates with audiences and contributes to the growth of your personal brand.

11. Optimize for Search Engines:
   - Implement basic search engine optimization (SEO) strategies on your website or blog to improve its visibility in search engine results. This can attract organic traffic and enhance your online presence.

12. Build an Email List:
   - Create an email list to directly connect with your audience. Use newsletters to share updates, exclusive content, and promotions related to your personal brand.

13. Online Courses or Workshops:
   - Consider creating online courses, workshops, or webinars that align with your expertise. This not only generates additional income but also positions you as an authority in your field.

14. Publish a Book or E-book:
   - If you have valuable insights or a unique story to share, consider publishing a book or e-book. This can establish you as an expert and provide additional revenue streams.

15. Monitor Analytics and Adjust:
   - Regularly analyze analytics and performance metrics across platforms. Understand what content resonates most with your audience and adjust your strategy accordingly to strengthen your personal brand.

Building a personal brand beyond TikTok involves a holistic approach, incorporating various platforms and strategies to create a cohesive and memorable online presence. Consistency, authenticity, and a commitment to providing value are key elements in the ongoing development of your personal brand.

Overcoming Challenges

Dealing with Algorithm Changes

Adapting to algorithm changes is a common challenge for content creators on platforms like TikTok. Algorithms are dynamic and can undergo updates, impacting the visibility and reach of your content. Here are strategies to deal with algorithm changes:

1. Stay Informed:
- Keep yourself informed about platform updates and algorithm changes. Follow official announcements, blogs, or forums related to TikTok to understand the modifications in the algorithm.

2. Diversify Content:
- Create diverse and engaging content that aligns with your niche. The algorithm may favor certain types of content at different times, so having a variety can help you stay relevant.

3. Adapt Quickly:
- As soon as you notice an algorithm change, be prepared to adapt your content strategy. Stay agile and experiment with different content formats, styles, and trends to see what resonates in the new algorithmic landscape.

4. Analyze Performance Metrics:
- Regularly analyze performance metrics such as reach, engagement, and follower growth. Understand how your content is performing after an algorithm change and adjust your strategy based on the data.

5. Engage with Trends:
- Engage with current trends and challenges. The algorithm often prioritizes content that aligns with popular trends, making it more likely to appear on users' For You Pages.

6. Consistent Posting Schedule:
- Maintain a consistent posting schedule. Algorithms tend to favor creators who post regularly, and consistency can contribute to your content's visibility.

7. Utilize TikTok Analytics:
- Use TikTok Analytics to gain insights into your audience, top-performing content, and follower demographics. This data can guide your content strategy and help you adapt to algorithmic changes effectively.

8. Collaborate with Other Creators:
- Collaborate with other creators on the platform. Collaborations can introduce your content to new audiences and enhance your visibility even during algorithm shifts.

9. Understand User Behavior:

- Understand the behavior of TikTok users. The algorithm prioritizes content based on user interactions, so creating content that encourages likes, comments, and shares can positively impact its visibility.

10. Quality Over Quantity:
   - Prioritize quality over quantity. While consistent posting is important, high-quality, engaging content tends to perform better in the long run, even with algorithm changes.

11. Build a Community:
   - Focus on building a community around your content. Engage with your audience through comments, duets, and collaborations. A strong community can support your content, regardless of algorithmic fluctuations.

12. Experiment with Content Length:
   - Experiment with different video lengths. The algorithm may prioritize shorter or longer videos at different times, so be open to adjusting your content length based on performance.

13. Embrace Change:
   - Accept that algorithm changes are a natural part of the social media landscape. Embrace the opportunity to evolve and refine your content strategy to meet the current preferences of the TikTok community.

14. Seek Feedback:
   - Seek feedback from your audience. Understanding their preferences and expectations can guide your content creation process and help you align with what the algorithm prioritizes.

15. Diversify Platforms:
   - Consider diversifying your presence across multiple platforms. While focusing on TikTok, having a presence on other platforms provides additional avenues for content visibility and audience growth.

Remember that adapting to algorithm changes is an ongoing process. By staying informed, analyzing data, and remaining flexible in your content strategy, you can navigate algorithmic shifts and continue to thrive on TikTok.

Success Stories

Success stories on TikTok often involve creators who have effectively navigated the platform's dynamics, connected with their audience, and achieved notable milestones. While individual success stories vary, here are some common themes and strategies seen in TikTok success stories:

1. Authenticity and Originality:

- Successful TikTok creators often prioritize authenticity and originality. They showcase their unique personalities, perspectives, and talents, creating content that resonates with viewers on a genuine level.

2. Niche Focus:

- Many successful creators carve out a niche for themselves on TikTok. By focusing on a specific theme, topic, or style of content, they attract a dedicated audience interested in that particular niche.

3. Engagement and Community Building:

- Building a strong sense of community is crucial for success. Successful TikTok creators actively engage with their audience through comments, likes, and duets. They make their followers feel valued and create a sense of belonging.

4. Consistent Posting Schedule:

- Consistency is key on TikTok. Creators who establish a regular posting schedule tend to maintain audience interest and visibility on the platform. Consistency also helps the algorithm recognize and promote their content.

5. Adaptability to Trends:

- Successful creators stay aware of the latest trends and challenges on TikTok. They adapt their content to incorporate trending sounds, effects, and concepts, ensuring that their videos align with the current interests of the platform's user base.

6. Quality Content Production:

- The production quality of TikTok content matters. Successful creators invest time and effort into creating visually appealing and well-edited videos. This doesn't necessarily mean high production costs; rather, it emphasizes creating content that looks polished and engaging.

7. Cross-Platform Promotion:

- Many TikTok success stories involve creators who leverage other social media platforms for cross-promotion. They share their TikTok content on Instagram, YouTube, Twitter, or other platforms to expand their audience and increase visibility.

8. Strategic Use of Hashtags:

- Successful creators understand the importance of using hashtags strategically. They incorporate trending and relevant hashtags to increase the discoverability of their content, making it more likely to land on the For You Page.

9. Interactive and Engaging Content:
- The best TikTok creators create content that encourages audience interaction. Polls, questions, challenges, and duets are examples of interactive elements that successful creators use to keep their audience engaged.

10. Strategic Collaborations:
- Collaborating with other creators can boost visibility and introduce your content to new audiences. Successful TikTok creators often engage in duets, collaborations, or shoutouts with others in their niche.

11. Monetization Strategies:
- Some TikTok creators turn their success into revenue by exploring various monetization options. This may include participating in the TikTok Creator Fund, securing brand deals, selling merchandise, or leveraging affiliate marketing.

12. Adaptation to Algorithm Changes:
- Successful creators adapt quickly to changes in the TikTok algorithm. They stay informed about updates, experiment with new features, and adjust their content strategy to align with the platform's evolving dynamics.

13. Storytelling Skills:
- The ability to tell compelling stories within the short-form video format of TikTok is a valuable skill. Creators who can captivate their audience through storytelling often stand out and build a loyal following.

14. Setting and Achieving Milestones:
- Successful TikTok creators set realistic milestones for themselves, whether it's reaching a certain follower count, achieving high engagement rates, or hitting specific content creation goals. Setting and celebrating milestones can contribute to long-term success.

15. Continuous Learning and Improvement:
- TikTok success stories often involve creators who are committed to continuous learning. They stay informed about platform trends,

analyze performance metrics, and adapt their strategies based on audience feedback and evolving trends.

While each success story is unique, these common themes and strategies highlight the key factors that contribute to success on TikTok. By incorporating these elements into your approach, you can enhance your chances of building a thriving presence on the platform.

Conclusion

In conclusion, TikTok has emerged as a dynamic platform that offers creators unique opportunities to express themselves, connect with a global audience, and even build successful careers. The platform's emphasis on short-form, engaging content has fueled the rise of diverse creators who have mastered the art of capturing attention and building communities.

The success on TikTok is often attributed to a combination of factors, including authenticity, niche focus, engagement with the audience, and adaptability to trends and algorithm changes. Creators who consistently produce high-quality, relatable, and innovative content tend to thrive, while those who actively participate in the TikTok community and leverage emerging features stay ahead of the curve.

Cross-platform promotion, collaborations, and strategic use of features like hashtags contribute to a creator's visibility beyond TikTok, expanding their reach and impact. As the platform continues to evolve, successful creators remain agile, embrace new features, and navigate algorithm changes with creativity and resilience.

For those aspiring to make a mark on TikTok, the key lies in finding your unique voice, understanding your audience, and staying attuned to the ever-evolving trends within the TikTok community. Whether you're aiming to entertain, educate, or inspire, TikTok provides a vibrant stage where creativity knows no bounds.

In the fast-paced and dynamic world of TikTok, success is a journey marked by consistent effort, adaptability, and a genuine connection with your audience. As you embark on your TikTok adventure, remember to be true to yourself, stay informed about platform developments, and most importantly, have fun expressing your creativity in this revolutionary digital space. The TikTok revolution is ongoing, and your unique contribution can be a part of shaping its future.